In Over my Head

How to Make Overthinking Work for You

NITHYA SUKILAN

gurucool
PUBLISHING

Published by:

Gurucool Publishing
#102, SaiKrupaNilayam,
Nagendra Nagar, Habsiguda, Hyderabad – 500
007 Ph: 040–69999200,
E-mail: info@gurucoolpublishing.com

Contact: nsukilan@gmail.com

ISBN: 978-93-93582-25-6

First Edition - 2022

Production Executive	: Madan Mohan R, Hyderabad
Cover Design by	: Nithya Sukilan
Printed at	: Devanshi Digital Printers Hyderabad

Printed at Manipal Technologies Limited, Manipal

In loving memory of my cousin brother Subodh Sudhakaran.

I dedicate this book to my parents, my greatest blessing from God, and my late cousin Subodh for being the inspiration, not just behind the stories in this book but in my life as well.

Introduction

This book is about coping with overthinking and methods you can put into practice in daily life to find strength when dealing with setbacks and challenges in life and how you can capitalize on your overthinking nature to benefit from it.

The aim of this book is to help readers who suffer from depression and anxiety to be able to cope better with their negative thoughts and emotions using methods that have worked for the author on a personal level. Nithya shares concepts and approaches to handling negative thoughts as well as short stories inspired by true life events. Nithya sincerely hopes that with her wisdom and practical solutions, she is able to add value to the life of her readers, regardless of the status of their mental well-being. She hopes that readers will be able to tap into their inner strength to weather any storm that rocks their boat with the help of this book.

Contents

Introduction v

1. Embrace your unique self 1

1.1 Avoid Seeking Validation 1

1.2 Do not Fear being Different 10

1.3 Silence the bullies 22

1.4 The Story of the Meek and Quiet Naomi 30

2. Live in The Present 37

2.1 Focus on the journey 40

2.2 Forget the outcome 48

2.3 Have faith in the universe 55

2.4 The story of Adam and his anxiety issues 62

3. True Love Does Not Question Your Self-Worth 68

3.1 Self-respect 68

3.2 Know your worth 76

3.3 Relationship expectations 79

4. Finding Light in The Darkness 87

4.1 Challenging negative thoughts 87

4.2 Embrace Loneliness 93

4.3 Always be kind 96

4.4 Blooming of the Lotus from Within 103

1. Embrace your unique self

1.1 Avoid Seeking Validation

Validation is the desire to receive approval from others for our actions, opinions, and achievements. The first and foremost way to embrace one's unique self, is to stop seeking validation from other people. This can be challenging for anyone, and is easier said than done, because even as a child, our mind is wired in a way that when we accomplish something, we seek recognition and praise from our parents.

It is a universal phenomenon and, everyone, children and adults alike, want recognition and appreciation for their accomplishments and achievements. Validation by itself isn't completely bad. It serves to affirm and instil confidence in an individual and builds their self-esteem. Seeking validation from others only becomes an issue when it allows the opinions, recognition, and approval of others to overpower one's own feelings and sense of self-worth.

Internal vs External Validation

Internal validation is when you validate or approve of yourself by having positive thoughts based on your feelings. It serves to build your sense of self -worth and a strong identity instead of diving into criticism and resorting to harsh self-judgment and self-blame thereby sabotaging one's happiness.

On the other hand, external validation happens when others validate your feelings by expressing their approval, showering praise and appreciation, and complimenting your efforts, ideas, opinions, or actions, to name a few.

The key is to be able to strike a balance between internal and external validation. Lack of internal validation will lead one to look for it externally most of the time while a magnified level of internal validation will make us arrogant and vain.

Reasons we seek validation from others

The concept behind human motivation is that we as social creatures have a basic need for acceptance. Everyone wants to feel included and to be accepted according to the norms and standards that society has set. Validation simply feeds this need for acceptance. The more validation we receive externally, the greater the need for acceptance. This proves to be a vicious cycle for those who are unable to draw a balance between internal and external validation.

Seeking validation also stems from a lack of confidence or self-belief in an individual or in other words poor self-esteem. When an individual lacks confidence in themselves, they will not trust or value their own judgment or opinions thus causing them to rely upon external validation from others as they place the opinion of others above their own. On the other hand, where internal self-validation is evident and a person is sure about themselves, they will not seek and thirst for external validation but simply acknowledge validation from others, if it happens.

Another reason why some people seek validation more than others is their childhood upbringing. Even as adults, our childhood upbringing is crucial in the development of the inner child in us. Adults who come from dysfunctional or broken homes, or have been abused as a child have a higher tendency to develop a needy inner child that craves approval from others and tend to grow up becoming people-pleasers. However, this isn't always the case. Some people are more prone to seeking validation due to their inherent personality type or co-dependency traits.

The people we seek validation from

The very first people we begin to seek validation from, right from our childhood are our parents. As infants and children, we seek eye contact and attention from them and cry or fuss if this need isn't fulfilled.

As we enter adolescence, friends become the centre of our universe and we seek validation from our social circle. With the transition into adulthood and working life, the need for validation shifts and we now seek it from our co-workers and superiors. We strive to perform our best at work to impress our bosses and steer away from work-related politics trying to be in everyone's good books.

Validation from relatives and family members is also sought after by trying to outperform others in the family via our professional or personal achievements. More often than not, this happens because we do not want to be compared to others who haven't achieved much in life and take it upon ourselves to set the bar high.

Last but not the least, we seek validation from social media. The 'like' buttons scream validation at its best. Social media platforms such as Facebook, Instagram, Snapchat, Clubhouse, Twitter, LinkedIn, and so on have made it possible for the public to view posts over the internet millions of miles across the globe. This opens the room for judgement and for critics to comment and show approval or disapproval of the person involved. Seeking validation via social media can be dangerous especially for teens and young adults as they are more vulnerable to cyberbullies who feed on this very strong need of theirs.

Ways for you to stop seeking validation

It's important to notice where your need for validation stems from. When you discover the motive behind seeking validation, it is easier to overcome the need for seeking it. For example, if your need for validation stems from poor self-esteem, you need to focus on developing this aspect of your personality, so that ultimately, you stop seeking external validation.

It is also crucial that you go down memory lane, to notice if your childhood and early development experiences may have a role to play in your validation-seeking behaviour.

Childhood neglect, abuse, or trauma may also contribute to the development of a needy inner child within us that often seeks validation from others.

In order to stop the habit of seeking validation, it is vital for us to make peace with rejection. It is important to understand that not everyone will support or be in favour of our opinions, achievements, and actions. Rejection can be reframed as a positive event when we consider it as feedback.

We should use it to mould ourselves to become better, and perform better in the future. Rejection, if viewed as a form of feedback can help us push our boundaries and not stay confined within our comfort zone.

It is also essential to our development that we cultivate a growth mindset, wherein we ensure a balance between positive and negative thoughts. It involves embracing compliments without letting it cloud our thinking and judgement, and accepting criticism without being deflated by it. When we prioritize self-development and constant learning, we are said to have a growth mindset.

Reasons to stop seeking validation

Ironically in this era of social media, many have resorted to masking and framing their identity on the internet in an attempt to seek validation and approval from others. Eventually, seeking validation externally paves way for anxiety and depression due to the pressure of outperforming others. For example, with the advancement of social media, body-shaming has become far more common than it used to be. The appearance of many 'key-board warriors' who reach out to social media to defame or criticize individuals who do not fit into social media or celebrity body size standards has grown by leaps and bounds.

The constant desire to seek validation from others, also disempowers our decision-making ability. We need to trust ourselves to leverage our own opinions and preference and not resort to becoming a people pleaser and rely completely on the opinion of others.

It is reasonable to seek the opinion of others when making a decision for ourselves. However, relying completely on others for approval and acceptance indicates that we don't trust ourselves enough to follow our gut instinct and this disconnects us from our intuition.

The need for validation also results in us giving our power away to others thereby losing our value as individuals. Others have power over us as long as we give away our power to them. It is only, if we stop leaning on others to validate us, and have faith in our abilities and know our worth, can we avoid disappointments.

1.2 Do not Fear being Different

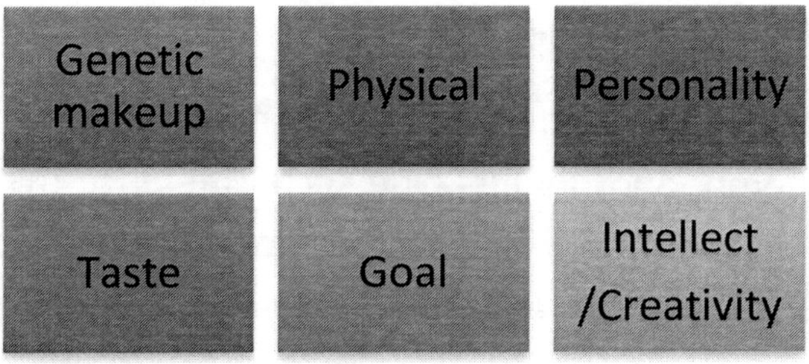

The meaning behind being different

Being different or unique means to be one of a kind and not having anyone else exhibit the same qualities as you, in terms of your actions, appearance, or speech. Sometimes, you may admire the style of a celebrity or that of a friend and try to imitate them but despite all your best efforts, you will not look like them, even though you may have the same clothes on, for you will appear uniquely different from them due to your physical attributes and body shape. The same is made more evident when you look at identical twins who may look alike or even seem to be carbon copies of each other, yet stand apart and reflect their own differences in terms of character, temperament, and personality.

There are many qualities that make a person different and unique. One such difference that can be distinguished at the molecular level is our genetic makeup. We receive our DNA from our parents and thus each one of us has a different genetic makeup. This is different even from our own siblings because we inherit different copies of each chromosome from each parent. The chromosomes that we inherit determines our gender, eye colour, skin tone, hair colour, and many other traits that make us different and unique as compared to others.

Another quality that makes us distinctive are our physical characteristics. No two individuals are created the same way physically. We have different physical qualities due to our ethnicity and nationalities resulting in unique shades of skin tone, hair colour, and eye colour, even if just a shade apart.

Our personality is also a quality that individualises us and sets us apart from others. The personality of an individual is moulded by their life events, experiences, and upbringing all of which differ from individual to individual. Some people have a bold personality and are more inclined towards being extroverts whilst others may have a meeker personality and tend to be introverts.

Even our personal taste in things such as clothing, food, and the people one spends time with, makes us different from others. For example, in most high schools, there is an obvious mixture of different races, and it has been observed that while some students are open to making multiracial friends, others stick to their own ethnic groups.

Another element that sets us apart from one another in a unique way are, our goals. Everyone has different goals in life. Even if two people have a similar career goal, their motivation behind that particular goal will differ. For example, Caron and Sanjay are best friends in medical school and their goal is to graduate as doctors. However, while Caron's motivation is to provide medical care for the underprivileged income group, Sanjay's motivation is to earn enough money to start his own medical centre. Your intellect or level of creativity is another criterion that can make you stand out as an individual, different from others.

As humans, we are either left-brained or right-brained dominant people. This is based on the theory brought to light by Nobel Prize winner Roger W. Sperry, a psychobiologic research scientist back in the 1960s.

He discovered and reiterated that people are either left-brained or right-brained dominant. If a person is mostly analytical in thinking, they are said to be left-brained whilst if a person is more creative or artistic, they are considered right-brained. According to Sperry's research, the left brain is associated with logic, sequencing, linear thinking, mathematics, facts, and words whilst the right brain is associated with imagination, holistic thinking, intuition, arts, rhythm, nonverbal cues, and daydreaming.

The perks of being different

You can be true to yourself

In a world of yellow LEGOs, you are a blue Lego which means you stand out in a crowd and there is nothing wrong with it. By doing so, you are being true to yourself and are making sure that you get noticed because, let's face it, who wants to be like everyone else, whether it's the matter of a crazy hairstyle or an amazing fashion sense that isn't trendy as on date. However, thinking outside the box and being different makes you more interesting and unique.

The biggest mistake one can commit, is to try and–attempt to 'fit in' just to keep up with societal norms and integrate with a group of people. Life has a habit of throwing circumstances at you that will eventually reveal your true self to others. So as much as you try to fake it to 'fit in', it will eventually show.

Being different allows you the freedom to be true to yourself because knowing and accepting that you are unique in your own way can be truly liberating. Staying true to yourself means you display the courage to stand up for who you are despite your belief or way of life that makes you different than the societal norm.

Less stressful

When you come to terms and accept yourself as being unique and an individual in your own right, life becomes less stressful because you don't have to worry about having your fake persona exposed. You no longer have to lie, pretend or fake your way through every day, trying to impress people who probably don't deserve to be a priority in your life.

You develop true and lasting relationships

Life as we know has a way of unravelling the layers of an individual with the passage of time. Staying true to yourself despite being different, shows others that you are a person of integrity and honesty accompanied with strong set of beliefs. This will naturally make you gravitate towards building true and lasting relationships because if people can accept you for who you are and still stick around, they love you for the 'real' you.

Increases your creative potential

When you see the world differently from others, you will feel free to explore the way things such as art and music make you feel. You will be able to see the reason you look at music or art and love it, hate it, or get bored of it. This in turn helps you to dig deeper into your soul and explore ideas that resonate with others because you are able to help the world see things from another perspective.

To cite an example, if you were to ask or observe any creative genius in history, you will realize that the first part of creating a masterpiece is knowing what you want and what you like. Then following through with what you think sounds, looks, or feels the best for you on a personal level.

You contribute more to the world

'If you judge a fish by its ability to climb a tree, it will live its whole life believing it's stupid'

- Albert Einstein

Have you ever heard of a child who would prefer to own a box of black crayons because it is classic? Of course not! Children love colours and they are oblivious to any trends, much less keeping up with those trends. This should be applied to life too. Stop depriving the world of your vibrant personality and unique attributes by masking it as part of the trend you want to be part of. The world needs you, and that includes YOU in all your flawed glory!

Take, for example, Albert Einstein, the most influential physicist in the 20th century. He loved mathematics and science but disliked grammar and had problems with spellings because he was dyslexic. However, his flaws did not stop him from discovering the 'Theory of Relativity'. If Einstein had given in and taken up literature as part of his education, his intelligence would've gone to waste and he probably wouldn't have been able to contribute to the world as he did. As the quote above mentions, if you judge a fish by its ability to climb a tree, it will live its whole life believing it's stupid which basically means it is absurd to judge the ability of everyone along the same metrics without taking into account their individual strengths and weaknesses.

Helps increase self-esteem

'You alone are enough; you have nothing to prove to anybody'

- Maya Angelou

When you learn to accept and embrace that you are different, you will discover, as the quote above so aptly states; that being yourself is truly enough and you don't need not try and be someone else just to prove yourself. This will increase your sense of self-worth and along the way boost your self-esteem as well, because you realize that people want to befriend you for your true self. They value your opinions as well as your behaviour and actions, which aren't bound by anyone else's expectations. For example, in the story narrated below, when Naomi accepts that she's highly intelligent and an introvert, she realises that she is enough and she need not pine for the approval of others in the name of friendship as her actions are no longer bound by the expectations of the popular students in school.

Prepares you for greater success

On clearing a job interview, value is given to the candidate who has something extra to offer, specifically in terms of their individuality and unique attributes. When you are different and have the ability to think and live outside the box, you should not let other people's judgment and opinion get in the way of your progress. Some of the most innovative and successful people in the world such as Steve Jobs, co-founder of Apple Inc., became successful because he was different and was able to not conform to another's definition of innovation.

Most companies hiring staff nowadays value having a variety of employees, each with his/her own set of personality in a job setting as this will give the work culture a better balance.

You have the power to say no when you need to

The unwillingness to be disliked or considered different often pressurises people to make decisions they would normally prefer not to. For example, you often hear about teenagers succumbing to peer pressure to try drugs. When a person is oblivious to being included in a group, they will not succumb to peer pressure and they will have the power to say no and live life on their own terms. Therefore, it is essential to accept and embrace your unique qualities in order to set clear and healthy boundaries for yourself.

You will have fewer regrets

Being different increases your creative potential where you make decisions based on what you like and feel, that fits you best. Chances are, these are the decisions that you will regret the least because even if you fail in your attempt, you will be happy knowing fully well that you did your best and won't be nagged by the 'what if' question. In fact, in your failed attempt, because the decision was made by you and based on your true feelings, you stay motivated to keep trying and not give up right away.

1.3 Silence the bullies

Bullying

Bullying is a pattern of repeated and deliberate harming, threatening and humiliating others who are smaller, weaker, or in any way more vulnerable than the bully.

Grounds for bullying

People bully because it's an effective method of getting what they want, as they may lack the social skills required to get things done otherwise. Bullying also establishes social dominance in a group and is a form of intimidation towards newcomers. Such behaviour develops at an early age when the normal aggression and tantrums of a toddler are not handled with care and these very children grow up to become bullies.

Bullies lack pro-social behaviour and empathy, are not troubled by anxiety, and therefore fail to understand other people's feelings. More often than not, chronic bullies usually come from broken homes and have a strained relationship with their parents or foster care, where they may have been abused, resulting in a deep trauma that becomes the root cause of their aggression and hostility.

Types of bullying

Physical bullying

Physical bullying is the most common type of bullying and happens when bullies use physical force or action to gain power and control over their victims. Physical bullies are usually bigger and stronger than their targets. Examples of physical bullying are kicking, hitting, punching, slapping, shoving, and other forms of physical threats. Physical bullying is the easiest type of bullying to be identified.

This form of bullying is given more attention to in universities, schools, and colleges as most of these educational institutions now have a low tolerance for physical bullying compared to other forms of bullying due to the loss of lives from physical injury attributed to bullying.

Verbal bullying

Verbal bullying is the use of words, statements, and labels to gain power and control over a victim. A typical verbal bully uses insults to belittle, degrade and hurt their victim. Victims become targets because of the way they look, behave, their social status, or disabilities if any.

This form of bullying is often harder to identify because attacks often occur when teachers or parents are not around, and consequently, there is no proof and finally it turns out to be one person's word against the other. Many underestimate the consequence of verbal bullying, which in the long run can leave deep emotional scars and affect the victim's self-esteem and performance in school, at work or even their personal lives.

Social bullying or Relational aggression

This type of bullying, also known as emotional bullying often goes unnoticed. Social bullying or relational aggression is a type of social manipulation where bullies hurt their victims by sabotaging their social standing. This type of bullying is more common amongst girls than boys where bullies ostracize their victims from a social group, spread rumours, and manipulate circumstances so that they are able to increase their own social standing while being in control of others. Think of it as the mean girl group you encountered (if any) in high school. They are the relational bullies. The victims are often insulted, ignored, excluded, threatened, or intimidated. Relational aggression is not limited to schools and universities but is also commonly encountered at the workplace.

Cyberbullying

Cyberbullying happens when a person uses the internet, a smartphone, or other technological devices to harass, threaten or humiliate their victim. Examples of cyberbullying include posting defaming images, making online defaming comments or remarks, threats, or sending hurtful emails or texts. Cyberbullying is becoming more widespread with the emergence of the social media era which makes data more easily accessible online and also makes it easier for cyberbullies to get away with bullying as they can simply create fake identities online and not risk being caught.

Cyberbullies usually post things online because they lack the courage to say it face-to-face. Technology gives cyberbullies the power of anonymity, thus giving them access to their victims anytime and anywhere with just a few clicks of a button.

Prejudicial bullying

Prejudicial bullying is said to occur when the bullying is based on prejudice towards people of different races or religions. This type of bullying can be severe and may escalate to violence and hate crimes.

Strategy to silence the bullies

Be or appear confident

Bullies feed off the lack of courage or fear in their victims and that is what gives them their power. In order to handle bullies, you need to target this power, because they lose their power when you stand your ground. Bullies are doubtful about deserving your respect deep down, and when you speak confidently with self-assurance, and a firm but respectful demeanour, they will eventually back off. Therefore, it is important to appear confident, even if you aren't feeling it within because the mere show of it helps ward off the bullies.

Get connected

Bullies often target victims who are alone or who lack a good social circle. Therefore, it is essential to get connected with others and build a good social support system. Try to maintain your relations with faithful friends and supportive adults. If you can't seem to establish good friendships, join a club or a society where you are more at ease and more likely to meet like-minded individuals who may share the same interests as you thus establishing common ground for a budding friendship.

Be strong, not emotional

Letting your emotions take over may escalate bullying because the bully will perceive this as a sign of weakness. Crying and showing emotions are signs of strength, but not in the eyes of a bully. Keep this in mind, the next time you encounter a bully. Always remember to keep your emotions in check in front of a bully. If you find it hard to do so, try a breathing exercise. Breath in through your nose for 3 seconds, hold your breath for 2 seconds and exhale through your mouth. Repeat this at least three times till your emotions are in check.

Don't let them cross your limits

Everyone has a limit of what they define as respect, and crossing that is taken as disrespect. It is important to set limits against the bullies and remain vigilant and assert yourself when they try to cross those limits. Tell them off politely, without getting emotional, that you don't appreciate their actions or speech. It will be helpful to practice your response in order to be more prepared in the event of another bullying situation arising.

Take action by reporting

Bullies often test waters by labelling, teasing, and starting off with minor physical attacks which progressively worsen when they notice the victim is unlikely to report them or stand up for their rights. Thus, it is advisable to report any form of bullying to higher authorities and nip it in the bud, in order not to encourage further bullying.

Take a Step back

Avoid reacting in the heat of the moment. Sometimes, it is wiser to wait it out instead of exchanging hostilities at that moment in time. This will give you time to think of a solution while the bully is busy ruining their own reputation in front of others.

1.4 The Story of the Meek and Quiet Naomi

Naomi, a high school student of mixed parentage; was born to a Caucasian mother and a Black American father. As a result of her mixed parental gene, Naomi was dusky in terms of skin colour. She was painfully shy and lacked confidence right since elementary school. She was meek, quiet, and often stayed aloof from other kids her age. It wasn't that she didn't like to socialize or make friends, but rather she saw herself as someone who wouldn't fit in with the crowd.

This got worse for her when her parents moved to The United Kingdom and she started high school. The other kids started teasing her for being different as besides having dusky skin, Naomi was also suffering from a skin disorder called Vitiligo which causes loss of skin colour resulting in pale whitish patches of skin colour surrounded by normal skin colour. This condition further sabotaged her confidence. She noticed other kids staring at her, and calling her names such as 'Dalmatian',

'Blacka' and 'Freak-show'. Kids at school would avoid sitting next to her as they were afraid of catching whatever she had.

After the beginning of the school term, and over the period of few months, she somehow had managed to make just three friends, but she was better off having no friends as these girls were friends with a group of bullies as well, who never failed to torment Naomi, every chance they got. Anna, their leader would order Naomi's 'friends' to do favours for them, as part of their initiation, in order to accept her into the group. However, despite succumbing to their tall and atrocious orders and carrying out the allotted tasks diligently, they would never keep their end of the bargain and finally, just cut her off with laughs and insults time and again.

There was this one instance, out of many other such incidents, when Naomi was asked to organize and make finger food for Anna's birthday party. Being the good girl she was, and keen to win their approval of the mean girls, she followed through with organizing, decorating, and making finger food for the party. She even spent her personal allowance, on getting the ingredients in the hope of being invited to the party as promised. She also bought a beautiful summer party dress which cost her a fortune.

However, as expected and true to her nature, in the end Anna just shrugged, smirked and said "Good, you are done! Run along now, Naomi. I'm sorry I've already exceeded the number of people I can accommodate, so maybe next time I'll allow you to attend one of my parties ....". This validation-seeking behaviour went on for about a year until Naomi could take it no more. Finally, it was in the third year of high school that she finally came to terms with the fact that they weren't her true friends after all. She needed to call a spade a spade and stop humiliating herself and risking losing all of her self-respect by craving and yearning for their approval.

It was the start of a new chapter in her life and Naomi started embracing her unique attributes and being comfortable in her own skin. Needless to say, it didn't happen overnight, but gradually she learnt to love herself and accept herself for who she was and what she was capable of.

For years she had secretly been aspiring to be a public speaker and saw this as a golden opportunity. She left her 'friends' and joined the Public Speaking Club in her high school, a club where students learn how to speak articulately, fluently and above all, confidently, in front of an audience. Joining the club boosted her morale because she began associating with like-minded individuals who shared the same love for speaking and thus, she started building healthy friendships with them.

The Club had a rule, that no member should be treated with disrespect and all members should encourage and be supportive of each other's efforts. This rule resonated with Naomi because after all the negativity she had gone through the past year, she needed all the support she could get. The club members inspired Naomi and encouraged and coaxed her to speak her mind and voice the challenges she faced as a student in high school. They neither judged her for her appearance nor questioned her. On the contrary, they accepted her as she was.

With practice, Naomi got better at public speaking and began honing her communication skills. She realized that it's okay to be different and that she need not fear it. Naomi had a goal, for she didn't join the club to just develop herself personally, she wanted to help others who were like her old self -meek, submissive and always seeing validation from others. She wanted to be the voice of the students and to silence the bullies. Gradually, with the help of her friend, Damien, they started a YouTube Channel that helped them manifest their dream. They interviewed parents, teachers, local celebrities, and key speakers on topics like bullying, be it in school or at the workplace. The response was overwhelming and they got a massive number of viewers and subscribers on the channel. Naomi got noticed and came under the spotlight. A local Mental Health Advocate from a non-profit mental health organization requested her to be the key speaker for their 'Mental Health Matters-Stop Bullying Campaign'.

Ecstatic and over the moon over the offer, Naomi was more than happy to oblige. She was also asked to participate in a brief photoshoot as well, with the purpose of spreading awareness and marketing the campaign. Where others saw flaws and blemishes, these people beauty saw reflected in those very flaws. This resonated strongly with the target audience of the campaign. After successfully participating in the campaign as a speaker and a role model, Naomi received another offer to speak at the prestigious stage of the TEDx event held in London. This was not just a dream come true for Naomi, but a huge milestone for her school as well, which had never produced a student worthy of the TEDx stage. Naomi was making history, not just for herself and her family but for her community as well.

Naomi was now popular at school and within her community. The mean girl's group, who had earlier scorned, rebuked and made fun of her didn't dare mess with her now, because she was assertive and confident of herself.

At the end of the final year of high school, Naomi was crowned 'queen valedictorian' for achieving outstanding grades, for her overall performance in public speaking, and her contribution to the community by representing the school at an international event. Amongst the audience, stood Naomi's bullies, watching her shine in all her glory. For once, they had nothing to say because she had silenced them with her success.

2. Live in The Present

The secret of health for both mind and body are not to mourn for the past, worry about the future, or anticipate troubles, but to live in the present moment wisely and earnestly'

- Buddha

More often than not, you tend to overthink everything because your mind is either too busy fixated with the past or the future. You fail to live in the present moment and appreciate its beauty because you are too busy worrying about things that have not happened yet or things that have happened to you before and left you scarred for life.

You can shift this pattern of overthinking by choosing to live and focus on the present moment. Take each step as it comes, instead of running and fumbling when things get too overwhelming. It is important to focus on the journey ahead, instead of fixating on the destination that lies ahead. This is one of the best ways grow and develop yourself as an individual.

The meaning of living in the present moment

Existing in the present moment of the 'here and now' means that you are fully aware, and acknowledge the events and environment around you at that very moment. You are not distracted by memories of the past and you don't worry about the future for your attention is centred on nothing but the present moment only.

Rationale to live in the present

Being in a present state of mind is essential for good health and happiness. It helps overcome anxiety, reduces worrying, and allows you to stay grounded and connected to yourself and your environment.

Leading this way of life is backed by scientific research as well. Living in the moment can also help us deal with setbacks and grief more effectively and greatly reduce stress levels, thereby enabling us to cope with negative emotions such as fear, sadness, and anger that harm our body and spirit.

Challenges of living in the present

- You are always prone to think about the future or dwell in the past. For example, advertisements, messages, and notifications on your phone are often associated with the past or future. Even checking your phone notifications while immersed in your work, takes you down memory lane or leaves you daydreaming thus losing out on the moment at hand.
- You often tend to exclude the not so pleasant part of your experiences to make your past seem rosier than it really was.
- You face uncertainty when you are living in the present which causes undue anxiety.
- Your mind simply likes to wander!

2.1 Focus on the journey

So how do you live in the present? By focusing on the journey of your life, of course!

Approaches on how to be Present and Focus on the journey

Here are some helpful tips to follow that will go a long way, if practiced regularly to help you focus on the journey of life:

If for some reason you do need to think about the past, do it in small doses and ensure that you are reminiscing about the past for a valid reason. For example, reliving a pleasant memory, to identify a mistake you made in the past so that you can rectify it, or looking out for patterns of past successes, are a few good reasons.

Similarly, if you start deliberating about the future, do it in small bits as well. Ensure that you are thinking about the future in a healthy way, keeping stress and anxiety at a minimum. Avoid worrying and instead allow yourself to think about it for a short while just to prepare for it and then come right back to the present moment and instead on delving on it, see how you can improve the given moment.

Practice makes perfect! Keep practicing the habits mentioned above and you will be on your way to leading a blissful life. It is important to note that, by living in the present, we are not ignoring thoughts about the future or past, but simply striking a delicate balance by not dwelling on those thoughts for longer than we should.

Gradually, over a period of time, you will notice that when you are aware of the present, you won't worry about being tangled in between thoughts of the past or have anxiety about the future. In fact, you will be able to revisit your past and anticipate the future without losing yourself in either one.

To live in the present, you need to focus on the journey but not the destination. With that being said, it does not mean you should not have a destination in mind, but rather emphasize and make an effort to get to the destination that you have already identified.

Your desired destination is the goal whilst the journey is how you intend to achieve that goal, and the experience and challenges you may face along your way.

Present Moment Awareness is the Antidote to Anxiety

Having present moment awareness will help you to worry less and thus reduce unnecessary anxiety.

Here are some helpful tips on how to increase your present moment awareness thereby reducing anxiety:

- Stop being self-conscious: Try to let go and avoid thinking about the outcome of your performance.
- Practice savouring the moment: Stop worrying about the future and the past

by maximizing your present moment experience.

- Bring your focus to your breath: Breathing exercises help an individual become more mindful, peaceful and make interaction with others easier.
- Go with the flow: Focus on gaining experience and make the most of the moment at hand by being engrossed in the journey
- Cultivate the ability to accept: This will help you to move forward rather than running away or living in denial about your problems.

Strategies to live in the present

Take notice of your environment

Let's be honest with ourselves! How often do we spend our day just looking at our surroundings and taking it all in?

After reading this page, I would like you to try this exercise for the next 5 to 10 minutes.

Try this exercise now!

Sit outdoors, close your eyes and take a deep breath. Now, slowly open your eyes and look at everything in your surroundings.

- What does the sky look like? Notice the shape of the clouds.
- What does the floor or the ground look like?
- Which animals do you see around you? What sounds can you hear? Are they loud or faint, in the far distance or close at hand? Observe and notice everything.
- What plants or trees do you see? What's the colour of their leaves?

Did you notice that you felt a lot calmer and more relaxed after this short exercise? It's because when you pause to take in your environment, you live in the present moment, which in effect means that you aren't burdened by thoughts of the past or the future.

Practice Gratitude

It is important to be grateful for what you have in your life right now because if your focus is fixed on things you don't have, you are more likely to get anxious, stressed, and worried. A proven way to practice gratitude is by keeping a gratitude journal to pen down a list of things you are grateful for and then review the list daily. Try writing at least three to ten things you are grateful for in your life right now and do it consistently and on a daily basis. You will soon come to realize; your life isn't half as bad as you assumed it to be because you have a lot to be grateful for!

Practice accepting things as they are

The key to living in the present moment is letting go of the need to control your situation. Accept the situation as it is and not the way you want it to be. You need to understand that you cannot control everything around you in life, and there will be situations in life when things need not necessarily turn out in your favour.

Practice Mindful Meditation

Mindful meditation helps you to become aware and improves your concentration. Practicing daily mindful meditation can help you to become more aware of your thoughts and feelings as you do things which will help you live in the present moment.

Spend time with loved ones

When you take out time and make an effort to be with your loved ones, it will help you garner positive energy and happiness. Consequently, when you are more positive, this further enables you to focus on the good in your life.

Go on a social media detox

Take a break from social media and all technology-based devices as this will help you stay grounded and more mindful of your surroundings. So, the next time you are at that dinner party, put down your phone and stop checking your social media and start being more present by socializing with people and taking in the environment around you!

2.2 Forget the outcome

Forget the outcome, Focus on the process

It is important to take note, that in goal setting, you need to be aware of the result or desired outcome. Nevertheless, your focus has to be on the process of getting there. You have to action oriented and accordingly inculcate the behavioural changes needed to achieve that goal.

For example, if your goal is to lose weight, instead of setting a goal that you need to lose 20 pounds, set a goal instead to exercise an hour a day, every day for 6 months in order to achieve your desired weight. This will make your goal more realistic more desirable and fun to achieve. Similarly, if you're aiming to write a book, set a goal to complete penning down 1000 words a day instead of focusing on how well your book will do in the market.

Strategies to focus on the process and not the outcome

Here's a 3-step method that you can use to shift your focus from the end result to the process itself to achieve that. This can be done by finding things you enjoy about the process:

Step 1: Identify anything you like about the process

It often becomes hard to focus on the process because you associate negativity with the process when faced with challenges. For example, studying poses a lot of potential negatives disguised as challenges, such as the requirement of intense concentration to retain information, the stress of attaining good grades, guilt from procrastination of studies, pressure from family, peers, and society to perform well, and last but not least an intense dislike of the subject. So how do you overcome this? You need to find something you like about studying! The idea may seem preposterous but think of anything, irrespective of however small it may be. You can focus on the positives such as the sense of satisfaction from acquiring new input and the feeling of achieving something productive for a day or you can resort to using coloured pens or highlighters to make graphic and colourful notes if you want your study material to be more visual.

Step 2: Concentrate on the component you like

Shift your attention to the component that you like whenever you do something. For example, while studying, concentrate on the satisfaction you get from seeing colourful notes besides comprehending and acquiring new knowledge.

Step 3: When your mind wanders, go back to what you like

When you find yourself thinking about the outcome, or elements of the process you don't like, shift your focus back to the things you like. For example, if, during the course of your studies, you begin thinking about getting good grades you might get stressed. At that time, make a conscious effort, to shift your focus back to what you like about the study material and relieve yourself from that stress. The things you like are anchors that shift your attention to the positives and make you stop worrying about the outcome. These very anchors also help motivate you throughout the process.

Practice repeating steps 1 to 3 for best results.

Reasons to focus on the process and forget the outcome

Gain the ability to deal with mistakes

Nobody is perfect, and mistakes are a part of life. Mistakes are essential for learning and growing in life. When you focus on the process, it gives you the ability to deal with mistakes better and makes you more willing to experiment and risk things, enabling you to progress towards a better outcome. On the contrary if your mind is too focused on the outcome, it will bring about anxiety and you will be less willing to risk making another attempt after a mistake or repeated failed attempts.

Satisfaction in pursuit of the outcome

You must have come across the age-old famous saying; 'Success is a journey and not the destination'. When you focus on the process or the journey as it's so rightly called, you are fully present in the here and now and therefore, you will be able to enjoy the experience of achieving your goal better, than if your focus was on merely the desired outcome. It keeps you engrossed and engaged and you're on the lookout for opportunities that come your way because it's all about learning and experiencing the whole process.

Fewer distractions

When you focus on the outcome, there is immense pressure to deliver outstanding results. You feel the need to prove a point by achieving the desired outcome. When you shift your focus to the process instead, you get rid of external distractions and feel less pressured by the outcome. Focusing on the process helps you to become a master in your pursuit because you are oblivious towards satisfying others and become more focused on yourself and your journey.

Gives you control over the situation

Having your focus on the outcome gives away your power, as you are focused on things that are beyond your control such as time, health and competitors. However, when you shift your focus on the process, it automatically boosts your self-esteem and empowers you to have more control over your thoughts and situation.

Provides a sense of fulfilment and happiness

Concentrating on the process, makes it more likely for you to enjoy the fruits of your labour even if things don't turn out in your favour because you persisted and were committed. Thus, to all intents and purposes, you are the winner, regardless of the real outcome. On the other hand, focusing on the outcome too much will only lead to frustration and disappointment when things don't turn out favourably. Thus, let your happiness be measured by the process and not by the desired outcome!

2.3 Have faith in the universe

In life, there are times when you will catch yourself saying 'I just have to trust the universe with this one!'. More often than not, you find yourself saying this when things feel too overwhelming. You will feel the need to surrender and let the universe take its course. Faith in the universe is a practice and an art that requires a tremendous amount of patience especially when you keep trusting the universe and believe that it will make it happen for you but you fail to see any results.

Here are 4 tips you need to keep in mind when you put your faith in the universe:

1. Understand the universe is within you

More often than not, when we put our faith in the universe, we assume there will be an external driving force that will intervene and save us from the troubles and setbacks in our lives. This is a false belief, as our strongest connection to the cosmos and our environment lies within us. When we put our faith entirely in the universe, we position ourselves to become dependent and disempowered from reality and living in a fantasy world.

2. Learn to let go but be practical

When you put your faith in the universe entirely, you subject yourself too much to the practice of 'letting go' hoping to be saved by it. It's important to let go sometimes, but you need to be practical and face your demons and fears yourself, as well as, get rid of the limiting beliefs that you may be holding onto. Growth happens when you stop hiding and start showing up and stepping up to face your setbacks. When your desire for change is bigger than your desire to remain in your comfort zone, amazing things happen.

Learn to let go of your fear, your doubts, and your limiting beliefs but be practical enough to take action and step up your game when there is a need for it.

3. The universe will serve you but not please you

How many times have you prayed for something, and did not get it? I am certain your answer is, many times! That's because God and the universe will serve you but will not necessarily, please you. Sometimes, our wish doesn't get fulfilled because it's probably not the right time for it to happen.

You have to put your faith in the universe and then trust that divine timing will take its course. Use that time to focus on and make the most of the opportunities that life and the universe has blessed you with. For example, most people pray for marriage and a loving life partner or soulmate, and when they get tired of looking for one, they put their faith in the universe to unite them with their twin flame, but often get frustrated when that doesn't happen. This is where divine timing comes into play. The universe will give you what you deserve when you are ready for it. You will find yourself finally meeting 'the person' when you least expect it because that is when you are deemed ready. So, stop expecting the universe to please you because if you do, you are paving the way for a huge disappointment!

4. Not getting what you want can be a gift

Sometimes, not getting what we want from the universe can be the greatest gift or a blessing in disguise especially if we are trying to opt for the easy way out. When faced with challenges and setbacks, we have no choice but to trust and rely on our innate abilities and strengths, and automatically we become less dependent on others to fulfil our needs. For example, a person who hopes and wishes to find their soulmate to fulfil their emotional needs will find the universe not giving them the opportunity to come across their soulmate until they have learned to fulfil themselves emotionally on their own. This, in turn, helps them to focus on other aspects of their life, such as career and personal development which prepares them for a happy life with their soulmate in the future.

The Route to putting your faith in the universe

By embracing powerlessness

If you think minutely, you may realize that you tend to shine brighter when you are helpless in a situation and have finally come to a point of surrender; especially more so when you realize that the odds are against you and out of or beyond your control. At that time, when you embrace the helplessness or powerlessness with a positive mind, you draw strength that you never knew you possessed in the first place, simply by surrendering and loosening your grip to control the situation.

Enhance Self-awareness

You need to be aware of your thoughts because your life is centred around what you think, feel and believe. When you put your faith in the universe, your thoughts need to be aligned with the universe. You must get rid of your limiting beliefs and focus only on positive thoughts in order to attract positivity into your life. You may have heard about the famous law of attraction which states that the universe returns to you what you give out. This means that if your thoughts and vibrations are positive, you will attract positive events into your life. Self-awareness can only come with the practice of mindful meditation. As you meditate more regularly, the nature of your thoughts will change and your faith in the universe will increase naturally and profoundly.

Learn from nature

Notice how abundant and generous nature is. Observe the beauty of nature all around you and the balance of it all. You may see yourself as a stranger on earth but you and your life were meant to exist right here, right now, on this very planet. Everything in nature has a purpose for its existence-the flowers and fruits provide pollen and seeds to produce another plant, the bees help to pollinate while the bacteria in the soil helps keep the soil fertile. The universe has a plan and a purpose for you too and it's your job to figure that out. Learn from nature and see yourself as part of the creation instead of observing externally and superficially.

A summary: The power of love from the universe

In short, the best method to have faith in the universe is to have faith in yourself. Instead of completely surrendering by letting go and thinking the universe will serve you, be practical and start stepping up to the game of life. Understand that the universe loves you by serving you with what is best for you at that moment in time and most importantly, trust divine timing. Never assume the universe–is there to please you. Understand that sometimes, not getting what you want can be a big blessing.

2.4 The story of Adam and his anxiety issues

Adam was a typical guy, an introvert, leading a mediocre life as a marketing and sales executive for a reputed multinational company in Vadodara, Gujarat in India. Besides being an introvert, he was also prone to social anxiety because of which he rarely mingled with his colleagues. His job was demanding as a sales executive, as he was required to meet new people and talk to them on a regular basis, and having frequent anxiety and panic attacks wasn't something to be proud of. While talking to the clients, mid-sentence he would start stammering, get flushed and start sweating. This was noticeable leading the clients to misunderstand, thinking something was amiss. Thus, more often than not they would back out from investing in the company. This was a major problem for Adam because the company had a monthly sales target that Adam needed to complete to get paid. As a result of his underperformance, he was regularly chided for being unprofessional and incapable.

The frequent bouts of anxiety continued affecting his work until one day, the company's Vice President, Subodh requested Adam to report to his office immediately. Subodh was recently appointed as the Vice President of the company, having been promoted from the position of Chief Executive Officer after 15 years of service. Subodh was known for his down-to-earth and benevolent nature and could often be seen mingling with people from different walks of life irrespective of whether they were -poor, rich, high-ranking officials or employees. Subodh never discriminated against nor undermined anyone. However, unaware of Subodh's nature, Adam was dreading his walk to Subodh's cubicle, thinking to himself that he might as well start packing his things because he was sure he was going to get fired this time.

When Adam finally arrived at Subodh's office door, he knocked sheepishly on the glass panel. "Come in", said Subodh firmly. Adam turned the doorknob and slowly let himself in and took the seat in front of Subodh. To Adam's astonishment, Subodh greeted him with a warm smile, which reduced his nervousness. Subodh then proceeded to fill a glass with water up to half its volume and put it in front of Adam while asking him firmly, "Ok Adam, tell me what do you see?" A little confused but calmer now, Adam replied spontaneously "I see a glass which is half empty". Subodh then added, "Hmmmm...interesting, I think I see the problem here". Adam just stared and before he knew it, he felt the sweat trickling down his forehead. He was having an anxiety attack again! Thoughts started racing through his mind about the likelihood of losing his job. Adam swallowed hard. Subodh noticed this and then gently said, "Relax, I am not going to fire you. I am just trying to understand things from your perspective. You see, Adam, an optimist sees the glass half full whilst a pessimist sees the glass half empty. Your answer told me that you seem to have a negative approach to things. Do you agree?"

Subodh then added gently, "Feel free to speak your mind and think of this as a friendly discussion between us". Adam nodded. He agreed with Subodh that he probably does think negatively at times. Subodh further continued saying, "I feel there's more to you than this negativity. It feels like you tend to get in your own way at times, do you agree? Tell me, what's bothering you, what is stopping you from performing well at work, Adam?" In reply, Adam confessed that he was diagnosed with anxiety issues when he was 17 years old and often had severe bouts of panic attacks that affected his life. It would surface the most at crucial times like when he needed to participate in presentations during college or when he needed to talk to clients at work.

After hearing Adam's explanation, Subodh replied calmly, "Adam, there, are three rules in life you should follow; One, focus on your journey, two, forget the outcome of your efforts, and three, have faith in the universe that things will always work for the better. You are anxious because you are not living in the present but too focused on the past and future". Subodh then added with conviction, "You worry about talking to clients and presentations because you put pressure on yourself regarding the outcome, and as a result, you lose the battle even before it begins. The next time you speak to a client, I want you to take a deep breath and tell yourself that your glass is half full and it is up to you to fill it further. You can do this! Don't think of them as clients but rather focus on adding value to their lives by getting to know them better and understanding their needs. This is what I mean by focusing on the journey. As you speak to more clients, you will get better and will be able to handle your anxiety better. Do not worry about closing the deal with clients, focus on the experience! That will get you where you need to be, and finally trust that the universe is with you in whatever effort you put in."

Adam took Subodh's advice and applied the three rules that Subodh had given him. To his surprise, Adam was soon able to manage his anxiety and emotions better and started performing well at work, even overachieving the monthly sales target. He soon got promoted as the head of the sales team. Adam was grateful to Subodh for believing in him and helping him climb the ladder of success. Subodh had indeed displayed the true traits of a leader and will always be an inspiration to others like Adam.

3. True Love Does Not Question Your Self-Worth

3.1 Self-respect

"Self-respect is the root of discipline: The sense of dignity grows with the ability to say no to oneself."

- Abraham Joshua Heschel

Self-respect and its importance

Self-respect is when a person values their own approach to living life, and makes life choices and decisions based on their unique personality. Self-respect is important because it is a gift to ourselves and makes us live life by being genuine. It's important because if you don't respect yourself and indulge in overly pleasing others then surely others will choose not to respect you either. Not having self-respect makes people take you for granted and treat you as if you were a door-mat.

Ego vs Self-respect

Ego fosters pride and leads one to make wrong decisions and actions in life whilst self-respect leads on to having self-control and confidence in any situation.

The difference	Ego	Self-respect
Feeling and thoughts	Only values their own feelings and thoughts	Values other people's feelings and thoughts
Behaviour towards others	Does not respect other people's opinions and undermines others	Team player and respects the opinions of others.
Motivation	Competition and winning	Personal growth and development
Fear factors	Failure and judgement from others	No fear

Emotions	Negative emotions such as anger, sadness, frustration	Positive emotions such as happiness and gratitude
Results	Generally, cause others to dislike them	People enjoy their company

Approaches to build self-respect

Here are a few tips that you can act on to start building your self-respect:

Identify your core values

Each and every action of yours should be aligned with your values and these in turn should stem from your authenticity because it is your values that will become the foundation for your actions and thoughts. For example, you are offered a lucrative job but it requires you to work with a boss with questionable integrity and morals that does not align with your core values, and you decide to turn down the offer, regardless of the income – it shows that you have self-respect.

Develop your vision

After identifying your values, you need to spend time working on how you can apply those values in real life. You need to identify who you are as a person, what you want in life, and ways to achieve your goal by identifying ideals for your life in every aspect such as career, relationships, and personal life. Having a clear vision will help you set clear boundaries with disrespectful people and keep them from sabotaging your journey to success.

Prioritize your mental and emotional needs

In order to build self-respect, it is important to ensure that your own emotional and mental needs are a priority over that of others. If you resort to people-pleasing, in the long run, you will eventually burn out and create room for unnecessary conflicts that may be detrimental to your mental well-being. It is important to be mindful and concerned about others' feelings but always be sure to have your interest in mind first before you help others and definitely not at the expense of your own wellbeing. If you've noticed, on a flight, the flight attendant tells us to attend to our oxygen mask first before assisting others under our care. Similarly, we need to put our needs first before attending to others.

Set boundaries

You tend to attract people who reflect your state of mind into your life. If you don't have self-respect, you will most likely associate yourself with people who don't respect you either. It is essential to set boundaries in any relationship that serves as an indication to others you value yourself and they need to respect you. For example, if your life partner wants you to change something about yourself that you don't feel comfortable changing, you should voice it out and explain why you are resisting. If the person still insists that you change for them, don't entertain their emotional manipulation. Instead, know where you stand and communicate your boundaries to them.

Be assertive

You need to take note when people are disrespectful and stop them then and there itself. Stand your ground firmly and be bold enough to tell them that their behaviour is disrespectful and unacceptable to you. For example, when your boss demeans you, you should be assertive and let your boss know that you find his or her language inappropriate and discourteous and that you don't appreciate it.

Be realistic

In order to maintain your self-respect, you need to learn to deal with criticism by being realistic. Never take criticism personally and look at it from a detached point of view.

Set standards for yourself

Learn to accept yourself as you are and understand yourself better. Be aware of your own values, personality, likes, and dislikes. This will help you to build character and set standards for yourself so that you know what to look for and what you are deserving of when building friendships or even a relationship for that matter.

Practice forgiveness

Learn to forgive yourself and forgive others. Instead of holding grudges, learn to move on. When you practice forgiveness, you liberate yourself and display integrity and moreover, it shows people you are mature and respect yourself enough to walk away from situations that aren't beneficial to your mental well-being.

Practice self-love

When you love yourself, you are less likely to become a people pleaser and risk jeopardizing your self-respect. Practicing self-love is sometimes easier said than done but as the saying goes, practice makes perfect!

Give and get respect

You have to give respect to others in order to gain respect for yourself. When you look for the good in others, you are more likely to look for the good in yourself too.

Take responsibility

Remember that you are solely responsible for your life and so you're the one who needs to take action. Stop playing the victim or the blame game and step up by taking responsibility for all your choices and decisions.

3.2 Know your worth

Self-worth

Self-worth can be defined as the ability to value yourself in any given situation or relationship. Knowing your worth is vital before committing to a relationship because only when you value yourself, will you understand and be aware of what you deserve and how you should be treated in a relationship. In other words, recognising your self-worth helps you set relationship standards and look out for red flags in a potential life partner.

Strategies to increase self-worth

Understand that your bank balance, job designation, outer appearance, and social media following does not determine your value! Although people around us and society in general place a high value on money, status, and fame, you do not need to succumb to the pressure of chasing money and fame. Instead focus your attention on what truly matters in life such as kindness, empathy, respect, and compassion for others, and let this become the mantra that defines who you are.

Work on and try to challenge your inner critical voice—When you find your critical inner voice talking too loudly, take a pause and analyse it. Ask yourself if your inner critic is being kind or not, whether it's really necessary and helping you and, if look out for evidence to support the claim. If the answer to all that is no, it's best to ignore the inner critic in you. Challenge your inner critic by reminding yourself that you are worthy, regardless of what you achieve or do not achieve in life.

Importance of self-worth in relationships

People with low self-esteem often base their self-worth on their relationship. This is the biggest mistake one can make because you are giving the other person the power to determine your self-worth. Instead, develop the ability to feel good about yourself regardless of being in a relationship or not.

Never allow another person, even if it's a loved one, to determine your value. Whether you are single, casually dating, in a relationship, or married, you should understand that you are always worthy of love and respect.

When you base your self-worth on another person, you will find it harder to deal with grief and breakups, if it is fated to happen, because then you will feel even more worthless and would have to start to build up your sense of worth from scratch and this can be devastating, to say the least. Having a healthy dose of self-worth will also work wonders in building new relationships. It's essential to love yourself first before loving another because loving yourself and knowing your worth will always bring out the best in you and help you to be able to love someone else better.

3.3 Relationship expectations

We are often advised not to set expectations in a relationship because expectations create room for discontentment, dissatisfaction and lead to conflict. However, having a healthy dose of expectations in a relationship ensures that we have a healthy rapport with our partner. Just be mindful to have realistic expectations and to communicate these clearly in order to strengthen the foundation of your relationship.

Approaches to Set Relationship Expectations

Here are a few things to be mindful of when determining expectations in a relationship:

Take the subtle approach

Never hand over a long list of your expectations to a person and expect them to deliver results. Be subtle, focus and explain what's important to you in a relationship, such as the values that you hold onto. It is also important to understand that, when you set expectations, do remember to ask what your partner expects from you as well. After all, nothing is one way and you need to give importance to their likes and dislikes as well.

Communicate clearly

Never drop vague hints about your expectations. Instead, set realistic expectations and communicate them clearly in a crisp manner. For instance, very often we see the lack of clear communication between two people in a relationship when one partner is constantly demanding time and attention. Gradually the other partner starts feeling smothered. However, had the expectations been communicated clearly in the beginning, this conflict could have been avoided.

Working together

It's important to understand that expectations are a two-way process and both you and your partner have the need to be heard and understood. You should work together in setting expectations in a relationship by discussing what is acceptable and what isn't and, how far are you both willing to go for the sake of your relationship. For instance, instead of expecting your partner to cook every day for you after work, make an attempt to pitch in by chopping up some veggies or helping out with the dishes.

Be realistic

It's important to separate the realistic from the unrealistic when setting expectations in a relationship. For example, being unacceptable towards infidelity is a realistic expectation but expecting flowers every day from your partner is an unrealistic expectation that is best to let go of.

Have an open mind

It is crucial to keep an open mind when setting expectations in a relationship because there are bound to be clashes and opposing opinions when discussing expectations. A safe bet would be to view things from your partner's perspective as well instead of countering it at every instance. This will in turn enable you to reach common ground and keep the peace.

Realistic expectations in a relationship

Showing affection

It is important to understand and accept each other's love language as a realistic expectation in a relationship. However, you should refrain from judging and defining how your partner expresses their love and affection towards you. Realistic expectation in terms of showing affection is to be caring, loving, and affectionate. However, you should never expect your partner to say 'I love you' a thousand times to you or engage in PDA (Public Display of Affection) because different people have different levels of comfort when it comes to displaying affection.

Honesty

It is important to discuss what honesty means to you and your partner and to honour it in order to build a strong and healthy relationship. This is a non-negotiable expectation because a lack of honesty often leads to infidelity. You should know and be able to share your past relationships, about your social circle, how close you are to your friends, and your relationship with your family without being pressured to reveal intricate details about your relationship with your ex or expecting to hear the same from your partner's past relationship.

It is also not absolutely necessary to share passwords unless you and your partner don't see a problem in doing so.

Trust

It is important to cultivate mutual trust between one another when in a relationship. You and your partner should be trustworthy and avoid being suspicious, insecure, and jealous. When you have mutual trust in a relationship, it doesn't leave room for insecurities and suspicion. However, you should also be mindful not to take advantage in the name of mutual trust.

Compassion

It's completely normal to expect your partner to be your source of comfort when you have had a bad day or when you are feeling low. However, it is unrealistic to expect your partner to read your mind when you are on the outs. Unless you express yourself, you cannot expect your partner to come to your rescue or rescue or solve your problem for you.

Respect for each other

The hallmark of a healthy relationship is respect for each other. Never let yourself be disrespected or treated like a doormat. When you respect your partner, it shows that you value your partner's perspective even if you don't necessarily agree with them. When respect is mutual, there is a better understanding and approach to solving conflict and arguments without the need of belittling one another. A realistic expectation can be to respect each other's feelings and involve each other in decision-making. However, you should never throw tantrums or bring up arguments, with the notion that your partner will deal with it in the name of respect for you.

Making time for each other

Spending quality time together is essential to bond and get closer. It helps a couple grow together. A realistic expectation, in this case, would be to expect your partner to make plans with you to spend time together. However, you should never expect your partner to spend every waking moment with you or never to make any plans that do not include you in it.

Personal space

Personal space is important in a relationship in order to sustain the independence and individuality of both partners in a relationship. If there is no personal space, it will lead to a co-dependency pattern of relationship which is not healthy. Both partners in a relationship need to have their own life and social circle, apart from a common one, and respect and value time away from each other.

4. Finding Light in The Darkness

4.1 Challenging negative thoughts

In order to manage your negative thoughts, you need to first recognize your thought pattern. Some common negative thought patterns include:

- Black and white thinking which is observing everything as one way or another and not in between.
- Personalizing, which is taking the blame for anything that goes wrong.
- Filter thinking, which is choosing to see things from a negative perspective.
- Catastrophizing, which is assuming the worst is going to happen in any situation.

Next, you need to find ways to challenge these negative thought patterns. For instance, when you have a negative thought, pause for a moment and evaluate if it is true and if there is any benefit from thinking that way. You can also challenge these thoughts by looking at them subjectively by role-playing as a friend who is giving advice to another person who had the same negative thought bother them. Think about what you would say to them to make them feel better, or give them an alternative approach to the negative thought and then apply the same to your own thoughts.

Another way is to take a break from negative thoughts. Try to dissociate yourself from it by allowing it only to stay in your mind for no more than five minutes and then take a break from it for the rest of the day and move on with your daily routine.

Challenging negative thoughts also comes naturally when we liberate ourselves from judgment. As human beings, judging ourselves and others is natural. We constantly compare ourselves to others which breeds dissatisfaction. A technique you can use the next time you feel constrained by judgments is to practice positive judgment. So, the next time you notice yourself judging a person or yourself, look for a positive perspective too.

Then there is the practice of gratitude that most of us have heard of and is one of the most widely used methods to challenge negative thoughts. There is no doubt, this method comes up most of the time because research has shown that feeling and expressing gratitude has a tremendous impact on our level of happiness and positivity. Being grateful even for small things on a daily basis can provide a sense of comfort to a person having a rough day for it makes you happy and keeps you motivated. Keep a gratitude journal and write in it on a daily basis as it can be an effective way to challenge negative thoughts that weigh you down. Trust me on this, I have one too! Practicing gratitude has numerous benefits, other than challenging negative thoughts. I have written more on this earlier under the topic 'Strategies to live in the present as well.

It is also crucial to shift your attention to your strengths when dealing with negative thoughts. We often find ourselves dwelling on the negatives which in turn leads us to undermine the positives. When you practice focusing on your strengths instead of your flaws, over a period of time, it will become effortless to feel positive and you will have a clear direction in life.

Lastly, if you feel that none of these methods resonate with you, do not hesitate or feel ashamed to seek—professional help from a licensed counsellor or a clinical psychologist. Seeking professional help can help you deal with negative emotions and thoughts that affect your quality of life. Therapy can also help to weather changes in life, help you deal with grief and loss and also assist in self-growth.

Feed your mind

You may have heard of the phrase 'You are what you eat' which means that what you consume becomes part of your body. To sustain and build a strong body, we need nutritious food. Similarly, the mind too needs to be fed with positive thoughts to keep it healthy. In order to find happiness in life, we need to control the chatterbox mind and develop a sense of calmness within us. For instance, if you are–on a vacation but your mind is in constant turmoil about your work, you will never find joy and be able to enjoy your holiday. Without a sense of inner peace life loses its lustre.

Here are some effective ways you can feed your mind with positivity and avoid overthinking:

1. Go to bed early and rise early.

2. Start and end your day with meditation.

3. Have a personal mantra and recite it whenever you get anxious or find yourself overthinking.

4. Do some reading that uplifts your mood on a daily basis.

5. Spend time with people who embody qualities you aspire to have.

6. Make healthy choices, especially when watching television or engaging in social media as what you feed your subconscious mind lingers with you.

4.2 Embrace Loneliness

Most of us have experienced feeling lonely at some point in our lives and let's face it, it's not the most uplifting feeling. However, being alone doesn't mean you should feel lonely. Loneliness in itself can help by allowing you to set aside that time to get to know yourself better and reflect on your values and preferences in your own time and space without any distractions or external noise.

Loneliness can be a trigger to overthinking at times too because when we are alone, our mind tends to wander and we tend to get critical and over analyse situations in our lives. However, when you take the step to embrace loneliness, you will find that you become a lot calmer and your thoughts will be more rational.

Here are a few ways you can embrace loneliness:

Get expressive-Let your emotions take control when you are lonely. Allow yourself to feel your loneliness 100% and observe your emotions and sensations. Take note of the thoughts that cross your mind when you feel lonely and cry if you need to let it out. Allow yourself to feel the discomfort and get comfortable feeling the discomfort.

Be silent-Silence can be scary for some of us because it is not what we are used to. We are so used to our hectic lifestyle and the noise that comes with it. Set aside some time every day to stay quiet. You can also pick up a hobby that you are passionate about that requires you to be in the zone of silence. As you do this activity, try to take in everything around you and appreciate the silence.

Practice mindful meditation-You can practice mindful meditation by simply being aligned with your senses, thoughts, and emotions without controlling or changing them. Practice mindful meditation for at least 5 minutes gradually building it up to 20 or 30 minutes a day while repeating positive affirmations to yourself that can keep lonely feelings at bay.

4.3 Always be kind

We should always practice being kind to others as well as ourselves.

"Carry out a random act of kindness, with no expectation of reward, safe in the knowledge that one day someone might do the same for you."

- Princess Diana

It's important to be kind because the practice of being kind towards other people and ourselves too helps alleviate stress levels and results in positive mental and physical changes. Being kind also increases the production of feel-good hormones such as dopamine, oxytocin, and serotonin. This further boosts the immune system and reduces blood pressure. It decreases the load of overthinking that in turn diminishes anxiety and depression, an inherent cause for many diseases.

Ways to be kind to yourself

Make time for yourself-One way you can be kind to yourself is by making time to do things that bring you joy and peace. It can be anything from writing, drawing, journaling, to playing a musical instrument, cooking, or even cleaning. This gives you the opportunity to rest and recuperate from your frantic work-life.

Acknowledge your achievements- You might notice that you often acknowledge the achievements of others but fail to do the same for yourself. Get into the habit of giving recognition to yourself too because you deserve it. Whenever you achieve something in life, give yourself a pat on the back, compliment yourself or you can even treat yourself to a gift that you normally wouldn't have bought.

This does not mean you have to be vain and show off to others but simply appreciate your achievements to keep yourself motivated to achieve more.

Silence the inner critic-You can silence your inner critic by summoning your positive inner conscience. This positive inner conscience's role is to challenge your inner critic every time it tries to demean you. Practice positive self-talk by capitalizing on your inner conscience.

Practice self-forgiveness-Sometimes in life, things don't turn out the way we want them to but that doesn't mean you should start blaming yourself. Instead, make a resolution to start over and forgive yourself for what happened in the past.

Take care of yourself-To be kind to yourself, you need to ensure you have adequate sleep, have a balanced diet with lots of fruits and vegetables, and exercise regularly. You also need to look after your appearance and groom yourself well.

Pamper yourself-Every once in a while, it's good to go on a retail therapy and buy yourself something really nice or pamper yourself at the nail salon, spa, go out with friends for a meal or even just have a warm soak in the tub surrounded by scented candles over the weekend.

Accept yourself as you are-By accepting yourself as you are, you allow yourself to fully express who you are and not let setbacks or challenges hold you back from moving forward.

Approaches to practice kindness towards others in everyday life

Be a good listener- Listening and showing interest during a conversation shows the other person that they matter and what they say is important to you. It's important to not interrupt while they are speaking and acknowledge that you are listening. Listening to someone who is sharing their feelings with you will also comfort them and make them realize that people do care about them.

Express compassion-When listening to a person, it's also important to display compassion by communicating to them that you understand their perspective on the issue because this will validate their feelings. It is important to show empathy and offer sound advice or sometimes simply be a shoulder to cry on in times of grief.

Give compliments-This is one of the easiest ways to express kindness. However, be sure to give genuine compliments and avoid using a sarcastic tone. A simple compliment given to a person who is having a rough day can brighten up their day and put a smile on their face.

Help someone- Offering to help someone without being asked is another act of kindness you can practice in everyday life. This can be as simple as holding the door open for someone who is carrying too many things to helping a blind person cross the road. Little acts of kindness like this can help ease someone's burden and though it might not seem like much to you, it goes a long way for the other person.

Say please and thank you-These are magical words and although they seem like two simple words, many people don't have the habit of using it especially when encountering people who offer paid services. This is because we assume that, since they are being paid, there is no need to say 'thank you '.

Little do we realise that a simple 'thank you' or 'please' will help brighten their day and even help build a rapport. It also strengthens the bond between two people, whether, in a marriage or any formal or informal relationship.

Smile more-Smiling at someone shows that you are warm and approachable besides being able to brighten someone's day. You will be surprised how a smile, even from a random stranger, can impact someone's day tremendously. Everyone is fighting their own battles and it gives them the ability to reflect on themselves on a bad day and build happier memories of that day.

Gift someone-The best gift you can give someone is to give them a handmade gift instead of a store-bought one. Doing this not only shows that you appreciate them but also shows that you took the time out and made the effort to think of them and customised it to make them feel special. However, if you can't find the time to make a handmade gift, you can even add a simple personalized note with a store-bought gift.

4.4 Blooming of the Lotus from Within

This is a story about Aparna, the daughter of a cleaner named Sunil who lived with his daughter in a slum in Mumbai. Sunil, on his death bed asks Aparna to sit next to him. He then weakly mutters her name and asks her to come closer. He had a crumpled piece of paper in his hand with a phone number and a name, 'Subodh' scribbled on it, that he hands over to her. Aparna looked at her father with mixed feelings. She was confused but also grieve stricken at the thought of losing her father any moment now Sunil muttered weakly, "Look for this man when I am gone , for he will be your guardian angel and guide in life. He is the reason behind your success in life." Having said that, he breathed his last. Aparna clutched her father's hand tightly as she cried her heart out.

Six months after Sunil's passing, Aparna cleared her Civil Services Examination with flying colours and was appointed as an Indian Administrative Service Officer by the state government. She was over the moon on her achievement but also saddened by the fact that her father was not around anymore to share her joy. Memories of her father came rushing back. She was fully aware of how hard her father had worked to finance her studies. Suddenly, she recalled the crumpled paper that Sunil had given her before he passed away. She searched for it high and low and finally found it neatly tucked away in her notebook. Aparna called the number that was written on it." Good morning, May I speak to Mr. Subodh Sudhakaran? I am Aparna," said Aparna warmly. To this Subodh replied with concern "Yes, Subodh speaking here, how may I help you, Aparna?" Aparna replied back calmly "No sir, there is no issue. I am just calling to ask you if we could meet up over a cup of coffee. My father, Sunil was a friend of yours and he gave me your number before he passed away. The meet-up is pertaining to that, it's more of a personal thing for me as I gave my word to my dad before he passed away". Subodh replied excitedly, "Oh! So, you're Sunil's daughter! Most certainly, we shall meet up. How about next Sunday at 5 pm at Cafe Coffee Day?" Aparna replied with contentment, "Sure, sir. Will see you next Sunday".

The following Sunday, Aparna met Subodh at the cafe. There was an awkward moment of silence between the two of them as they calmly took turns sipping their coffees respectively. Subodh then lamented," So, tell me, Aparna. What can I do for you? Sunil was a dear friend of mine and I am truly sorry for your loss". Aparna's eyes welled up with tears up as she tried her best to keep her emotions in check. She replied in a shaky voice, "My father told me something before he passed away. He gave me your name and number and told me to find you if I need guidance in life. He also said you were the reason behind my success. Is this true? I have come to seek answers." Subodh paused for a moment and then spoke with a warm smile, "If you need guidance, I am here to show you the way, but I can't give you the answer that you seek". Aparna nodded politely before she spoke," I just started my job and lately I have been struggling to clear myself of self-doubt. I never told anyone this, sir. I am having trouble and overthink my decisions. I put immense pressure on myself to perform well and often feel lost and alone without my father's presence in my life. He was my pillar. My strength. My everything".

Subodh replied gently "You see Aparna, the very fact that you have made it this far in life shows that you display true grit and that you were born to lead. Never doubt yourself. Always be kind to yourself as you are kind to others. Understand that nothing and nobody is permanent in life. We come into this world alone and we leave alone. You are your father's legacy and he lives on in you. Embrace loneliness, for the path to success is often a solitary one. Feed and nourish your mind with positive thoughts. Challenge your negative thoughts and watch the magic happen. Be like the lotus! Bloom and rise above the mud and darkness. Radiate into the world!". Aparna nodded and thanked Subodh for his timeless words of wisdom.

Subodh was not aware of how successful Aparna was. He was also clueless about her designation or job until her driver arrived in a government official car and the waiter told Subodh that she was a high-ranking Civil Services Officer that was serving the country. Subodh was taken aback, but nevertheless felt fulfilled that he had played a crucial role in helping her father finance her education.

That was the last time Aparna saw Subodh. Unfortunately, two months after their meet-up, Subodh too passed away of a heart attack. Aparna was devastated to hear of his passing and visited his family to convey her condolences. Nevertheless, Subodh's words and values stayed deeply etched in her heart. She wholeheartedly practiced what he had taught and finally bloomed from within, by acknowledging her true potential as a leader just like a lotus.

"IF YOU FEEL LOST, DISAPPOINTED, HESITANT, OR WEAK, RETURN TO YOURSELF, TO WHO YOU ARE, HERE AND NOW AND WHEN YOU GET THERE, YOU WILL DISCOVER YOURSELF, LIKE A LOTUS FLOWER IN FULL BLOOM, EVEN IN A MUDDY POND, BEAUTIFUL AND STRONG."

— MASARU EMOTO, SECRET LIFE OF WATER